How To Plan A
KWANZAA
Celebration
Ideas For Family, Community,
And Public Events

Ida Gamble-Gumbs   Bob Gumbs

CULTURAL EXPRESSIONS, INC. New York

Publisher's Cataloging-in-Publication
(Provided by Quality Books, Inc.)

Gamble-Gumbs, Ida
     How to plan a Kwanzaa celebration: ideas for family,
community and public events / Ida Gamble-Gumbs, Bob Gumbs
     -- 1st ed.
     p. cm.
     Includes bibliographical references.
     ISBN: 0-9629827-1-7

     1. Kwanzaa. 2. Afro-Americans--Social life and customs.
I. Gumbs, Bob. II. Title.

GT4403.G36 1998   394.261
                         QB198-790

CREDITS
Edited by Claire Harris
Cover art by Yvette Jenkins
Text illustrations pages pgs.5, 7, 17, 31, 53, 54 by Yvette Jenkins
Book design by Bob Gumbs
Layout and execution by Tari Design

ISBN: 0-9629827-1-7
Library of Congress Catalog Card Number: 98-93220
Printed in the United States of America

For Diallo, our son

Our nieces: Elveria, Henriann, Carolyn, Annie, Vivian, Kathy, Debbie, Brenda, Allyson, Marsha, Valerie, Nzingha, and Barbara

Our nephews: Michael, Flynn, Leslie, Curnell Jr., Larry, Fredric, Cedric, Wayne, Victor, Reggie, Andre, Derrick, and Bryan

Contents

About the Authors

Ida Gamble-Gumbs has been celebrating Kwanzaa for over 15 years. She has coordinated Kwanzaa celebrations in Washington, DC, Maryland, and South Carolina. Ida is also president of Cultural Expressions, Inc., a New York-based greeting card publisher specializing in Kwanzaa and other cards for African-Americans.

Bob Gumbs has been involved in the Black cultural movement since the 1950's and a Kwanzaa celebrant for over 15 years. Bob is president of Gumbs & Thomas Publishers, Inc., based in New York. Gumbs & Thomas publishes books on African-American history and culture, including four books on the subject of Kwanzaa. The company also distributes a variety of other Kwanzaa and multicultural products.

Acknowledgments

We would like to express our appreciation to the many individuals, organizations, and businesses for their contributions and cooperation in helping to make this book possible. We are most grateful to our families for their support throughout the entire writing of this manuscript.

Thanks to Mary Hickson, Ann Gamble and Inez Mallett for their honest comments and advice during the early stages of the manuscript. To Catherine Stephens for her willingness to read the recipes for clarity.

We are especially grateful to Dr. Dorothy I. Height and the National Council of Negro Women for granting us permission to reprint the Black Family Reunion Pledge, by Dr. Maya Angelou. To Malani Edwards and the Johnson family for granting us permission to reprint Lift Every Voice and Sing, words by James Weldon Johnson, music by J. Rosamond Johnson.

Special thanks to John Watusi Branch, Director of the Afrikan Poetry Theatre, The Reverend Dr. Otis Moss, Jr., Pastor of the Olivet Institutional Baptist Church, and Andrew P. Jackson (Sekou Molefi Baako), Executive Director of the Langston Hughes Community Library & Cultural Center who supplied programs of their Kwanzaa celebrations.

Many thanks to Dorothy Gamble, Ernie Wyatt, Joyce R. Broome, Beverly Green, Warren Barksdale, Harold Thomas, Cynthia Weathers, Hazel Parker, Martha Gamble, Betty Gilmore, Beverly Smith, Noill Martin, Essie Gamble, Francine McGill, Catherine Stephens, Inez Mallett and Ann Gamble who submitted their favorite recipes for inclusion in this book. Thanks to Mary Sligh for sharing a number of her hometown recipes. We wish also to express our appreciation to Patricia Mitchell, author of Soul On Rice, Kraft Creative Kitchens, Air Jamaica, and Amalgamated Publishers for granting us permission to reprint their recipes.

We are grateful to Nigerian Fabrics & Fashions and Fatou's Fashion Designs who contributed photographs of their beautiful African fashions. We are also grateful to Mary Hickson and Cedric McClester for giving us permission to reprint their poems.

We particularly wish to express our gratitude to our editor, Claire Harris, for her valuable editorial contributions. Our gratitude is also extended to Dr. Darryl S. Tukufu, president of The Tukufu Group, for his helpful insights on Kwanzaa celebrations.

To Josephine Clark, Hazel Parker, Joseph Gamble, Jr., Ron Campbell, and Cynthia Weathers, thanks for testing the recipes. To Marcee Bruton, thanks for your continued support throughout this process.

We wish to acknowledge Jose and Ayisha Ferrer and family for their continued dedication and commitment to promoting Kwanzaa and its values.

Finally, to Dr. Maulana Karenga, the creator of Kwanzaa, we extend our sincere thanks and appreciation for giving us the opportunity to celebrate ourselves.

Tutankhamun (seated) receiving Huy, governor of Ethiopia. Mural from tomb of Tutankhamun. Thebes. XVIIIth Dynasty.

Introduction

In recent years, Kwanzaa has experienced tremendous growth. The African-American holiday of family, community, and culture, created by Dr. Maulana Karenga in 1966, is now observed by millions of people of African descent. An increasing number of families, community organizations, churches, educational and cultural institutions, and individuals are having annual Kwanzaa celebrations.

Bob and I, along with our son Diallo, began observing Kwanzaa in our home during the 1980's. It was also around this time that we started attending private and public Kwanzaa celebrations in the New York City metropolitan area. Since 1993, my family (the Gambles) has held annual Kwanzaa celebrations.

The idea for a book on planning Kwanzaa celebrations was conceived during many hours of research, when I was coordinating my family's first celebration.

At a family reunion in South Carolina several years ago, there was a discussion about ways in which our family ties could be strengthened. Even though the Gamble family has always shared a certain closeness, there was a need to reach out to other relatives that we only saw at reunions. We also felt that the strong bond that we had experienced as children growing up in South Carolina was not necessarily shared by our offspring and other relatives of their generation.

The idea of having a Gamble family Kwanzaa celebration was suggested. We felt that this celebration would not only bring many of us together again at the end of the year, but would also introduce Kwanzaa and the Nguzo Saba (The Seven Principles) to other members of the family. The idea was accepted overwhelmingly.

Once the decision was made to have a Kwanzaa celebration, I assumed the responsibility for coordinating the event. Being aware that there would be family members participating in their first Kwanzaa celebration, I wanted to gather as much information about the holiday as possible. Presenting a program that was educational, as well as entertaining, was important.

Bob assisted me with my research on the holiday. We read a number of books that were written on the subject of Kwanzaa. I also consulted with individuals who had coordinated Kwanzaa events.

In keeping with the third principle of Kwanzaa, Ujima (Collective Work and Responsibility), I solicited the help of other family members in planning the program. Words cannot describe the excitement that was generated within the group as we planned our first celebration. There was an instant thirst to learn more about Kwanzaa.

On December 31, 1993, our extended family came together in the spirit of Umoja (Unity) at my sister's home in Washington, DC. There were thirty participants. For the first time, we shared libation, lit the candles, discussed the seven principles, feasted on a variety of foods, and celebrated our cultural heritage as a family.

How To Plan A Kwanzaa Celebration is based on my research and experience in planning the Gamble family celebrations. In this book, we have attempted to put together information needed to plan a successful family, community or public event. Even though we have provided general information on how Kwanzaa is celebrated, our main focus is the evening of the Karamu (feast).

In keeping with the fourth principle of Kwanzaa, Ujamaa (cooperative economics), we have also included a selected listing of community-based businesses in the United States and the Caribbean selling Kwanzaa products and African fashions.

It is our sincere hope that this book will inspire more people of African descent to observe the Kwanzaa holiday and celebrate our rich history and culture each year.

Ida Gamble-Gumbs
June, 1998

The Origin of Kwanzaa and the Nguzo Saba (The Seven Principles)

KWANZAA is the newest of the annual end-of-the-year holidays. It is now celebrated by millions of people in the United States and around the world.

The Origin of Kwanzaa

Kwanzaa, the African-American celebration of family, community, and culture, is observed from December 26th through January 1st of each year. The holiday was created in 1966 by Dr. Maulana Karenga, an activist-scholar and educator. "Kwanzaa", derived from the word "Kwanza" from the East African language of Kiswahili, is based on traditional African "first fruits" of the harvest celebrations.The extra letter "a" in Kwanzaa was added to accommodate the seven children who participated in the first Kwanzaa program. Kwanzaa is unique among American holidays because it is based on traditional African and African-American culture, not on historical figures or events.

Kwanzaa is a coming together of family, friends, and the community to celebrate our cultural heritage, pay tribute to the ancestors, and reinforce the bonds that unite us as a people.

In the early years, Kwanzaa was often thought of as a black Christmas, or as a substitute for Christmas. This is a misconception. According to Dr. Karenga, "Kwanzaa is not a religious holiday, but a cultural one with an inherent spiritual quality as with all major African celebrations." (*Kwanzaa: A Celebration of Family, Community and Culture,* by Maulana Karenga, pg. 122, *Commemorative Edition*). Today many African-Americans observe both holidays.

Kwanzaa is founded on seven principles called the Nguzo Saba. These principles, based on traditional African culture, form a value system that not

---

*Adinkra Symbol (Sankofa) of the wisdom in learning from the past to building for the future.

only builds and strengthens the world African community, but also serves as a catalyst that sustains us as a people. The seven principles are listed below. (See glossary in the back of this book for pronunciations.)

The Nguzo Saba (The Seven Principles)

1. **Umoja (Unity)**
   To strive for and maintain unity in the family, community, nation and race.
2. **Kujichagulia (Self-determination)**
   To define ourselves, name ourselves, create for ourselves, and speak for ourselves.
3. **Ujima (Collective Work and Responsibility)**
   To build and maintain our community together and make our brother's and sister's problems our problems and to solve them together.
4. **Ujamaa (Cooperative Economics)**
   To build and maintain our own stores, shops and other businesses and to profit from them together.
5. **Nia (Purpose)**
   To make our collective vocation the building and developing of our community in order to restore our people to their traditional greatness.
6. **Kuumba (Creativity)**
   To do always as much as we can, in the way we can, in order to leave our community more beautiful and beneficial than we inherited it.
7. **Imani (Faith)**
   To believe with all our heart in our people, our parents, our teachers, our leaders, and the righteousness and victory of our struggle.

Dr. Maulana Karenga

The Symbols of Kwanzaa

KWANZAA has seven basic and two supplementary symbols. Each represents traditional cultural values and concepts in the lives and struggles of African people. The basic symbols are

1. **Mazao (The Crops)**
   The symbol of traditional African harvest celebrations and the rewards of productive and collective labor within societies.
2. **Mkeka (The Place Mat)**
   The symbol of traditions, history, and the foundation of knowledge for the people.
3. **Kinara (The Candleholder)**
   The symbol of collective roots of the people.
4. **Muhindi (The Corn)**
   Symbolizes the children of the family and our hope in their future.
5. **Mishumaa Saba (The Seven Candles)**
   Symbolizes the Nguzo Saba, the value system on which the foundation of Kwanzaa is based. The seven candles are: one black (center), three red (left) and three green (right) candles.
6. **Kikombe Cha Umoja (The Unity Cup)**
   Symbolizes Umoja, the unity of the people, the first principle of Kwanzaa.
7. **Zawadi (The Gifts)**
   Symbolizes the labor and love of parents, and commitments made and kept by children.

The two supplemental symbols are

Bendera (Flag)

The colors of the Kwanzaa bendera are black, red and green. Black for the people, red for their struggle and green for the future and hope that comes from their struggle.

Nguzo Saba (The Seven Principles) Poster

Used for display at Kwanzaa ceremonies, the poster lists the seven principles.

Celebrating Kwanzaa

KWANZAA can be celebrated in various ways. According to Dr. Karenga, diversity of approaches is expected. He advises, however, that "this diversity must be within a framework that strengthens the holiday, not undermines it." We have listed below, a number of ways in which Kwanzaa is celebrated.

Kwanzaa Greetings

During Kwanzaa, celebrants greet each other by asking "Habari gani?" (What's the news?)

The answer is the principle for that particular day. For example, the answer for the first day of Kwanzaa would be "Umoja." The greeting "Heri za Kwanzaa" or "Happy Kwanzaa" can also be used.

Day 1, December 26th-**Umoja** (Unity)
Day 2, December 27th-**Kujichagulia** (Self-Determination)
Day 3, December 28th-**Ujima** (Collective Work and Responsibility)
Day 4, December 29th-**Ujamaa** (Cooperative Economics)
Day 5, December 30th-**Nia** (Purpose)
Day 6, December 31st-**Kuumba** (Creativity)
Day 7, January 1st- **Imani** (Faith)

Displaying Kwanzaa Symbols

The basic Kwanzaa symbols are displayed on a table covered with African fabric or a combination of black, red and green material. Seven candles (mishumaa saba), representing the Nguzo Saba, are arranged in the Kinara. One black candle is placed in the center, three red candles on the left, and three green candles on the right. Each day of Kwanzaa, beginning with the black candle, a candle is lit alternately from left to right to represent the principle for that day.

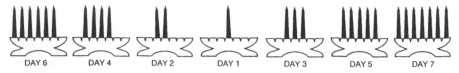

DAY 6   DAY 4   DAY 2   DAY 1   DAY 3   DAY 5   DAY 7

Family Celebrations

In the home, the principle for a particular day is discussed at mealtime, or at the time the candle is lit. A brief explanation of the principle is given by the person lighting the candle (preferably a child, if present). If children are present, it is important to give examples when discussing the principles.

Different cultural activities such as singing, poetry reading, and storytelling are often scheduled for children and adults during Kwanzaa. Families and individuals can also have their own Karamu (feast). See *Planning The Program* in the following chapter.

During Kwanzaa, children are rewarded with Zawadi (Gifts) for their good work and accomplishments during the year. These simple gifts should have some educational and cultural value, and may be handmade.

Community Celebrations

Community based organizations present Kwanzaa celebrations which include the history and meaning of the holiday, lighting of the Kwanzaa candles, explanation of the meaning of the symbols, and pouring of libation. Performances by cultural, musical and dance groups, as well as a Karamu (feast), may be included. Daily cultural activities, such as storytelling, poetry-reading, face-painting, and arts and crafts may also be scheduled.

Public Celebrations

Schools, universities, museums and libraries often plan different activities pertaining to African-American culture and history before and during Kwanzaa. Performances by African and African-American dance and singing groups are scheduled. Libraries also schedule storytelling and poetry-reading sessions and may show cultural films.

During the month of December, there is an annual Kwanzaa Fest held in New York City. Check your local newspaper and community calendar of activities for similar events in your city.

Other Activities

For information on pouring tambiko (libation), ancestral roll-call, and the harambee chant, see the chapter on *Planning Your Celebration: Planning The Program*.

In the following section, we offer ideas and suggestions for planning family, community, and public celebrations on the evening of the Karamu. Please keep in mind that this information may be modified to suit your situation.

Planning Your Celebration

ONCE the decision has been made to have a Kwanzaa celebration, someone must assume the responsibility for getting things started.

Planning activities and a program for the celebration can be time-consuming, depending upon the type of event you are having. At least four months should be allowed for planning communal or public celebrations. In larger cities, it may be necessary to begin preparations even earlier. Since family celebrations are usually not as formal or structured as communal or public events, two months should be ample time.

Committees

Even though it is not necessary to have a committee for every aspect of the celebration, there are certain committees that may be needed. They are: planning, program, decorating, and food.

The number of committee members should be kept to a minimum. Through experience, we have learned that the more people involved, the more difficult it is to reach decisions. It is also important to select individuals who are sincere about getting the job done and have the time to do so.

Even though we do not suggest forming a clean-up or break-down committee, it may be necessary to engage individuals in advance to take care of these duties. We do feel, however, that this should be a group effort.

Listed below are general duties and responsibilities of the various committees. Keep in mind that these duties may be re-assigned to different committees, if necessary.

The Planning Committee

The planning committee is responsible for setting a date, selecting a place for the celebration, establishing the costs, and advertising the event. In some situations, this committee might also assume the responsibility of planning the program. This committee should consist of the Kwanzaa celebration coordinator, co-coordinator, secretary, and financial secretary.

Setting A Date

Since Kwanzaa is celebrated during the height of the year-end holiday season, it is very important to establish a date for your celebration as soon as possible. Activities and programs may be scheduled at any time during the seven days of Kwanzaa. Some organizations and institutions schedule Pre-Kwanzaa celebrations.

Traditionally, the Karamu is held on December 31st. In some cases, however, the Karamu is scheduled for January 1st. In order to accommodate children and our elders, it may be a good idea to schedule the Karamu in the late afternoon or early evening.

Selecting A Place

If it is necessary to reserve or rent a place for your celebration, this should be done immediately after establishing a date. Keep in mind that there are many holiday activities taking place at this time of the year, and accommodations may be limited.

There are a number of options that may be considered, such as community and cultural centers, civic centers, schools, churches, private community rooms, and hotels. For a private or semi-private family celebration, the home of a family member would be ideal. The place selected should be large enough to accommodate the number of participants anticipated. A kitchen with stove, refrigerator, and possibly a microwave should be available, and in working condition. The lighting, sound system, and seating capacity should be checked before making a decision.

If it is necessary to rent additional chairs or tables, contact party and chair rental centers as early as possible. In emergency situations, try renting chairs from your local funeral home. If these items are rented, have a clear understanding of the return date and time, to avoid paying late charges.

In certain communities, it may be advisable to select a place that is accessible to public transportation, in case of inclement weather during the month of December.

Financing the Celebration

Your expenses may include rental services, food, decorations, printing cost, possible fees for performers and guest speaker, and other miscellaneous costs. Unless funds have been allocated in your budget for this type of event, thought should be given as to how expenses will be paid. If outside funding is needed, contact should be made with private and public sources immediately in order to determine their application deadline.

In family celebrations, it may be necessary to establish a certain amount of money to be contributed by individual family members or households. If this is done, someone should be selected to assume the responsibility of collecting the money. It is advisable to start the collection during the early planning stages.

For community or public celebrations, it may be necessary to ask participants for a small donation to help defray expenses.

The Program Committee

The program committee must plan and coordinate the Kwanzaa celebration program. They must also communicate with all scheduled performers and guest speakers and obtain their written commitment to participate in the program. A committee of three is sufficient. One person should be experienced in using a typewriter or computer.

Planning The Program

Allow enough time to plan a program that is informative, instructive, and educational, as well as entertaining. The karamu is a time for ceremonies, remembering, rejoicing, cultural expressions, and feasting. Cultural expressions should reflect traditional African culture, and the culture of the African diaspora in the form of music, dance, song, poetry, and drama.

The Kwanzaa celebration program generally consists of the following components: Welcome Statement, Ritual, Information, Karamu (feast), Cultural expressions, Distribution of Zawadi (gifts) and Tamshi La Tutaonana (Farewell Statement), and the Harambee chant.

Try using local talent, where possible, for your program. Check within your own community or city for talents such as African drummers, dance troupes, guest speakers, and singing groups. Contact should be made with these individuals or groups as soon as possible.

In planning your program, keep in mind that there may be guests in the audience that are participating in a Kwanzaa celebration for the first time. As a result, there are certain aspects of the ceremony (pouring libation, candle lighting, ancestral roll-call, and harambee chants) that should either be explained verbally by the person in charge, or as a written explanation in the program. Whenever audience participation is encouraged, information should be disseminated to all participants (libation statement, songs, poems, pledges, etc.) before the program begins. This information can be given to the participants as part of the program package. Through experience, we have learned that celebrations are more successful when the audience understands what is going on and becomes a part of it. The audience should be encouraged to participate in the libation, ancestral roll-call, discussion of Nguzo Saba, the harambee chant, and cultural expressions.

Libation (tambiko) is poured to honor our ancestors. Water or juice is placed in the unity cup (kikombe cha umoja), and poured in the directions of the four winds: north, south, east, and west. The leader then drinks from the cup and leads the group in a verbal Harambee (without raised hands). The cup is then passed among family members and guests. Each person either takes a sip from the cup, or makes a sipping gesture. It is recommended that a tamshi la tambiko (libation statement) be made as the libation is poured. (See page 25 for sample libation statement).

Raising the names of the ancestors (ancestral roll-call) is an important part of the ceremony. Dr. Karenga states, "At community or family celebrations of Kwanzaa, the historic or ancestral roll-call, i.e., calling out or raising the names of ancestral heroes, heroines and departed relatives is a meaningful and spiritually uplifting ritual." (*Kwanzaa: A Celebration of Family, Community, and Culture*, by Maulana Karenga, p. 94).

During the ancestral roll-call, the audience is encouraged to stand and call out the names of great men and women who dedicated their lives in the struggle for freedom and liberation of African people. The names of departed relatives and other individuals who have had a positive influence in the lives of others may also be called out at this time.

At the end of the program, the Tamshi La Tutaonana (farewell statement) is made. This statement is used to end the karamu and the year. (See page 26 for a sample farewell statement.) The person who makes the farewell statement should end the celebration by having the audience stand and lead them in the Harambee chant.

The Harambee chant (Let's all pull together) is usually repeated seven times, as a reinforcement of the seven principles. The Harambee is performed by raising the right arm, with hand open, above the head. Pull down, closing hand into a fist, while verbally saying Harambee (hah-RAHM-bay). This process is repeated five times. On the seventh Harambee, hold the first two syllables a little longer before pulling hand down into a fist. According to Dr. Karenga, the Harambee may be done at anytime to urge unity and collective work and struggle.

Even though lighting the mishumaa (candles) can be performed by anyone, it is recommended that children participate in this activity where possible. As the candles are lit, a brief explanation of the principle for that particular day should be given.

To assist you in planning your program, we have included a **Kwanzaa Celebration Program Format** on the following page.

Kwanzaa Celebration Program Format

Welcome Statement
A. Introduction and history of Kwanzaa
B. Recognition of distinguished guests and all elders

Ritual
A. Tamshi La Tambiko (The Libation Statement)*
B. Pouring of Tambiko (Libation)
C. Ancestral roll-call
D. Lighting of Mishumaa (Candles)
May be read as libation is poured

Information
A. Explanation of the meaning of each Kwanzaa symbol
B. Discussion of the Nguzo Saba (seven Kwanzaa principles)

Karamu (Feast)

Guest Speaker (Optional)

Cultural Expressions
A. Dancing, Singing, Drama, Poetry
B. Group singing (call and response)

Testimonials (Optional)

Distribution of Zawadi (Gifts)

Tamshi La Tutaonana (The Farewell Statement)

Harambee Chant (Repeat seven times)

Informing Prospective Participants

Once you have finished planning your celebration, you are ready to contact the participants. For family celebrations, contact can be made by telephone or written invitation. (See sample invitation below). Invitations should be mailed at least four weeks before the date of the celebration. This will give everyone time to plan their holiday activities.

Kwanzaa invitation designed by Ida Gamble-Gumbs for Cultural Expressions, Inc.

For community or public celebrations, contact should be made with the media to find out their deadline dates for listing community activities. Send a press release to your community or local newspaper. An announcement should be sent to radio and television stations. Flyers advertising the celebration can be distributed throughout the community. Your telephone number should be on all communications, in the event anyone needs additional information.

The Decorating Committee

This committee is responsible for gathering the Kwanzaa symbols and other decorations, setting up a Kwanzaa table, and putting up decorations.

The Kwanzaa Setting and Decorations

There are seven basic symbols and two supplementary symbols that are needed for the Kwanzaa setting. They are: Mazao (crops), Mkeka (mat), Kinara (candle holder), Muhindi (corn), Mishumaa Saba (seven candles), Kikombe Cha Umoja (unity cup), Zawadi (gifts). The supplementary symbols are: the Bendera (flag), and the Nguzo Saba (seven principles) poster or other representation.

As the number of Kwanzaa observers grows, these symbols become more difficult to find. They can be purchased from bookstores, gift shops or cultural shops in your community. If they are not available locally, check the Shoppers Guide For Kwanzaa Products in the back of this book for a store near you. You can also buy these symbols by mail from many businesses across the country.

You may also want to practice Kuumba (creativity), and make some of these symbols yourself. If they are handmade, children should be encouraged to help with them. *Let's Celebrate Kwanzaa: An Activity Book For Young Readers* (page 19), by Helen Davis-Thompson, gives instructions for making a Kwanzaa celebration set.

The Kwanzaa colors are black, red, and green, and should be dominant in an African decorative setting. African baskets, kente cloth, African-American and traditional African paintings and sculptures, and other arts and crafts may be used, as long they are in good taste, and contribute to the spirit of the holiday. Black, red, and green streamers can also be draped around the gathering place.

Usually decorations are put up in the home a week before Kwanzaa. Some people, however, prefer to wait until December 26th, in order to avoid any conflict with Christmas. If the celebration is held outside the home, allow enough time for putting up decorations. Start early on the day of the event, or, if possible, the night before.

The Kwanzaa table can be covered with a piece of African material or with a combination of black, red and green materials if African material is not available. Begin decorating by placing the mkeka (mat) on the table. The kinara with the mishumaa saba (seven candles) should be placed on the mkeka. Keep in mind, the black candle should be placed in the center of the kinara, the three red candles to the left, and the three green candles to the right. The kikombe cha umoja (unity cup), muhindi (ears of corn), mazao (crops), zawadi (gifts) should then be placed on the mkeka. The bendera (flag) and the Nguzo Saba poster should be placed near the Kwanzaa table.

Children should be encouraged to help with the decorations since this is a good time for them to learn about Kwanzaa. This decorating time can serve as teaching sessions, not only for children, but for adults as well. Each time a symbol is placed on the mkeka, there can be a brief discussion about that symbol. When the Nguzo Saba poster is hung, talk about the seven principles, and how they can be applied in our lives, not just at Kwanzaa, but throughout the year.

The Food Committee

Unless your Karamu is a catered affair, a public event with food vendors, or a small family celebration, a food committee is needed. This committee is responsible for planning a menu, purchasing food and paper supplies, preparing the food, and setting up for the feast. Since there is quite a bit of work involved in preparing food, your committee should consist of as many people as you feel are needed.

Traditionally, participants are asked to contribute prepared dishes for the Karamu. If possible, try getting commitments in advance from the participants to prepare certain dishes. In doing so, you will be certain of not only having enough food, but a variety of foods. In addition, the committee will have an idea as to how much food they will have to prepare themselves. For individuals that are unable to bring a prepared dish, items such as fruits and breads may be suggested.

For the Karamu, emphasis is placed on traditional foods that reflect our many cultures: African, Brazilian, Caribbean, Creole, and Southern. There should be an abundance of good, wholesome foods. The menu should be well-balanced and economical. *(Please see our chapter on recipes and basic menu suggestions).*

It is recommended that the food be set up in the center of the gathering place, so that it is convenient for self-serving.

Sample Kwanzaa Celebration Programs

ON the evening of the Karamu, families, friends and the community gather to pay tribute to the ancestors, share libation, light the Kwanzaa candles, and to enjoy singing, drumming, music, dancing and feasting on a variety of cultural dishes.

In this section, we have included sample Kwanzaa family, community, and public celebration programs that may be helpful in planning your event. A libation statement, farewell statement, the song, *"Lift Every Voice and Sing"*, *"The Black Family Reunion Pledge"*, and poems are also included. Keep in mind that these programs may be modified to accommodate your celebration.

In addition, we have listed ideas and suggestions for practicing the Nguzo Saba (seven principles) during the year.

The Gamble Family
First Annual Kwanzaa Celebration
December 31, 1993 6:00 P.M.

Musical Recording.."Kwanzaa" by Kent

Opening .... Adult

Prayer...Adult

Welcome ....Adult

Tribute to Ancestors ....Adult

Libation ....Leader/Audience
(The Libation and Harambee will be explained by the person in charge.)

Lighting of Mishumaa (candles) ....Children/Young Adults

Discussion of Nguzo Saba...Audience Participation
(A copy of the Nguzo Saba (Seven Principles) has been given to each person.
Please join in with the discussion of these principles)

Karamu (Feast)

Cultural Expressions...Audience Participation

Distribution of Zawadi (Gifts)..Audience Member

Farewell Statement/Prayer ....Adult

Harambee Chant ....Audience
Harambee! Harambee! Harambee! Harambee!
Harambee! Harambee! Ha Raam-m-m-m-Bee-e-e-e-e!

Note: Each person has received a copy of the Nguzo Saba (seven principles) and an explanation of the Kwanzaa symbols. Please teach them to your children, discuss them with other family members and friends, and practice the Nguzo Saba daily, throughout the year.

The Gamble Family
Fifth Annual Kwanzaa Celebration
January 1, 1998 4:00 P.M.

Musical Recording.."Drums of Passion" Olatunji

Opening Statement...Adult

Prayer..Adult

"Lift Every Voice and Sing"..Audience

Welcome/Recognition of guests..Adult

History and Origin of Kwanzaa...Adult

African Dance...Youth

Poem "Free"..Young Adult

Tamshi La Tambiko (Libation Statement)..................Audience participation

Libation..Elder/Audience participation

Ancestral Roll Call..Audience participation

Lighting of Mishumaa (Candles)..Young Adults

Discussion of Nguzo Saba (Seven Principles)............Young Adults/Audience

Explanation and Meaning of Kwanzaa Symbols....................................Adult

Family Tribute...Young Adult

Creative Dance..Youth

Presentations..Adult

Karamu (Feast)

Cultural Expressions..Audience participation

Farewell Remarks..Adult

Harambee (Repeat seven times)....................................Audience participation

Community Kwanzaa Celebration
Manning, South Carolina
January 1, 1995 4:00 P.M.

African Dance Presentation ....Children's Dance Group

Opening Statement ....Mistress of Ceremonies

Invocation...Elder

Recognition of Guests ....Adult

Musical Selection ....Adult

History and Origin of Kwanzaa ....Adult

Tamshi La Tambiko (Libation Statement) ....Adult/Audience

Pouring of Tambiko (Libation) ....Elder

Ancestral Roll Call ....Adult

Lighting of Mishumaa (Candles) ....Children Escorted by Young Adults

Discussion of Nguzo Saba (Seven Principles)....Adult Audience Participation

Speaker ....Guest Speaker

Karamu (Feast)

Presentations/Awards ....Adult

Cultural Expressions..Audience Participation

Closing Statement ....Adult

"Lift Every Voice and Sing" ....Audience

Harambee Chant ....Audience
Harambee! Harambee! Harambee! Harambee!
Harambee! Harambee! Ha Raam-m-m-m-Bee-e-e-e-e!

Queens Borough President Claire Shulman
in conjunction with
The Center For Culture
The Afrikan Poetry Theatre, Inc.
&
York College
present

A GALA KWANZAA CELEBRATION

Celebrating Ujima (Collective Work & Responsibility)
Sunday, December 28, 1997
2:00 p.m. - 8:00 p.m.
Enjoy our exciting African marketplace all day!

Program Part 1

Master of Ceremonies ....Fearone LaLande
2:00 p.m.- Welcome ....John Watusi Branch
Executive Director, Afrikan Poetry Theatre
2:10 p.m. - The History and Meaning of Kwanzaa.........John Watusi Branch
2:30 p.m. - Joy of Performing Workshop
3:00 p.m. - Matsimela Dance Company
3:30 p.m. - Redeemed Ministries & Steel Pan Sensation
4:00 p.m. - Greetings from Deputy Borough President Peter Magnani
4:05 p.m. - Greetings from Dr. Charles Kidd, President of York College
4:10 p.m. - Akeyne Baako African Folk Music Ensemble
4:40 p.m. - INTERMISSION

Program Part II

Mistress of Ceremonies...Louise Adelokiki
5:30 p.m. - Lighting of the candles, explanation of the Kwanzaa symbols,
and pouring of the libation ....John Watusi Branch and
the Afrikan Poetry Theatre children

5:50 p.m. - Devore Dance Company
6:20 p.m. - African Dimensions Collective Dance Company
6:50 p.m. - Sing Sing Rhythms Dance Co. from Senegal
7: 30 p.m. - Distribution of Zawadi to the Children
Fruit will be distributed on your way out

York College Performing Arts Center
94-45 Guy R. Brewer Boulevard
Jamaica, New York

Keepers of Faith, Hope and Heritage Ministry
Kwanzaa Celebration Program
December 30, 1997 7:00 P.M.

Opening ....Imani Dancers

Elders Processional...Children and Youth

Congregational Hymn.."Lift Every Voice and Sing"

Permission to Speak ....Adult

Welcome ....Adult

Statement of Kwanzaa Principles...Adult

Special Presentation..................................U.S.Postal Service Diversity Office

Selection ....Youth/Children Choirs

Libation Statement and Ceremony ....Pastor

Lighting of Candles ....Children and Youth Representatives

Ancestors' and Elders Prayer ....Deacon

African Family Pledge ....Adult

Offering/Selections ....The Voices of Olivet

Introduction of Speaker..Adult

Speaker...Guest Speaker

Altar Call for Children and Youth ....Pastor

Gifts to the Children

Harambee ....Adult
Escort of Elders to Feast Celebration in O.M. Hoover Center

Reprinted by permission of Olivet Institutional Baptist Church, Cleveland,Ohio,
The Reverend Dr.Otis Moss, Jr. Pastor.

Queens Borough Public Library

LANGSTON HUGHES

Community Library & Cultural Center

presents

13TH ANNUAL

KWANZAA
CELEBRATION

Saturday
December 13
10:00 a.m. - 9:00 p.m.

Florence E. Smith
Community Center
102-19 34 Avenue, Corona, Queens
(One block south of Northern Boulevard)

For additional information call:
Langston Hughes Community
Library & Cultural Center
718/651-1100

Andrew P. Jackson
(Sekou Molefi Baako)
Executive Director

Schedule of Events

10:00 a.m. – 9:00 p.m.	All Day Crafts Fair
1:00 p.m.	Opening Ceremony - The Meaning of Kwanzaa African Dimensions Collective
2:00 p.m.	Deidra Murray, Nikki Williams and the Langston Hughes Urban Griot Choir
3:00 p.m.	Linda Humes - "Kwanzaa: A Time to Celebrate"
4:00 p.m.	Latin-Jazz Coalition led by Demetrios Kasteris
5:00 p.m.	Melvin Hunter - Balladeer
6:00 p.m.	Al Bryant Quintet featuring Kym Lawrence

Admission is free   **It's a family celebration**

Funding is provided in part by the N.Y.S. Council on the Arts, N.Y.C. Department of Cultural Affairs, Queens Council on the Arts,
Meet The Composer - New Composers Program, the Queens Borough Public Library and the Library Action Committee of
Corona-East Elmhurst, Inc.

"LIFT EVERY VOICE AND SING"

Lift every voice and sing, till earth and heaven ring,
Ring with the harmonies of liberty; let our rejoicing rise,
High as the listening skies, let it resound loud as the rolling sea.
Sing a song full of the faith that the dark past has taught us,
Sing a song full of the hope that the present has brought us,
Facing the rising sun of the new day begun
Let us march on till victory is won.

Stony the road we trod, bitter the chastening rod,
Felt in the days when hope unborn had died; yet with a steady beat
Have not our weary feet, come to the place for which our fathers sighed?
We have come over a way that with tears has been watered,
We have come, treading our path through the blood of the slaughtered,
Out from the gloomy past, till now we stand at last,
Where the white gleam of our bright star is cast.

God of our weary years, God of our silent tears,
Thou who hast brought us thus far on the way;
Thou who hast by Thy might, led us into the light,
Keep us forever in the path, we pray.
Lest our feet stray from the places, our God, where we met Thee,
Lest, our hearts drunk with the wine of the world, we forget Thee;
Shadowed beneath Thy hand, may we forever stand.
True to our God, True to our native land.

Words by James Weldon Johnson
Music by J. Rosamond Johnson

Reprinted by permission of the Johnson Family.

TAMSHI LA TAMBIKO
(The Libation Statement)

For The Motherland cradle of civilization.
For the ancestors and their indomitable spirit.
For the elders from whom we can learn much.
For our youth who represent the promise for tomorrow.
For our people the original people.
For our struggle and in remembrance of those who have struggled on our behalf.
For Umoja the principle of unity which should guide us in all that we do.
For the creator who provides all things great and small.

Reprinted from "KWANZAA: Everything You Always Wanted To Know But Didn't Know Where to Ask", by Cedric McClester. Published by Gumbs & Thomas Publishers, Inc. New York.

TAMSHI LA TUTAONANA

(The Farewell Statement)

As we end the year, let us give thanks to the creator for the precious gift of life. Let us honor our ancestors for the contributions and sacrifices they made for freedom, justice, equality and the enlightenment of our people. Like the branches of a tree, let us reach out to each other in the spirit of unity and love. Let us resolve to serve as positive role models for our children, and lead by example. Let us continue to practice, and encourage our children and our friends to practice the seven principles of Kwanzaa; Umoja, Kujichagulia, Ujima, Ujamaa, Nia, Kuumba, and Imani throughout the year. As we begin a new year, let us commit ourselves to building a stronger sense of unity within our family and our community. Until we meet again at our next Kwanzaa celebration...

HARAMBEE !   HARAMBEE !   HARAMBEE !

HARAMBEE !   HARAMBEE !   HARAMBEE !

HARAMBEE !

BLACK FAMILY REUNION PLEDGE

Because we have forgotten our ancestors, our children no longer give us honor. Because we have lost the path our ancestors cleared kneeling in perilous undergrowth, our children cannot find their way. Because we have banished the God of our ancestors, our children cannot pray.

Because the old wails of our ancestors have faded beyond our hearing, our children cannot hear us crying. Because we have abandoned our wisdom of mothering and fathering, our befuddled children give birth to children they neither want nor understand.

Because we have forgotten how to love, the adversary is within our gates, and holds us up to the mirror of the world, shouting, "Regard the loveless."

Therefore, we pledge to bind ourselves again to one another.
To embrace our lowliest,
To keep company with our loneliest,
To educate our illiterate,
To feed our starving,
To clothe our ragged,
To do all good things, knowing that we are more than keepers of our brothers and sisters, we are our brothers and sisters.

In honor of those who toiled and implored God with golden tongues, and in gratitude to the same God who brought us out of hopeless desolation. We make this pledge.

Written expressly for the National Council of Negro Women
Black Family Reunion Celebration on May 14, 1986.
by Dr. Maya Angelou
(Used by permission of the National Council of Negro Women)

"FREE"

Freedom is more than just a condition that exists.

Freedom is the very essence of our being, and it moves from within us, out into our lives.

I free my mind of past hurt or negative thoughts and allow my soul to reach new heights of discovery.

I free my mind of limitations.

I am free to sow and magnify my potential to the maximum.

And if I happen to make mistakes, I consider them learning experiences that help me know that I can do better - next time.

I Am Free! I proudly proclaim, I Am Free!
Thank you, heart, body, mind, soul, and spirit.

I AM FREE!

Mary Hickson

"AFRICA'S GREAT LEGACY"

Africa's great legacy;
a torch that burns in you and me.
Our history a source of pride,
that lets us know, God's on our side.

A history not often told,
but one in which our people hold,
hegemony with all mankind,
it's written down for us to find.

Somewhere there's a history book,
so search it out, and take a look.
Store what you learn within your mind,
then pass that knowledge that you find.

After all is done and said,
our history lives, it isn't dead.
The pages written everyday
by each of us, in our own way.

How it will read, is up to us
And given this, each of us must,
remember history will view,
What we neglect, as well as do.

Cedric McClester

Reprinted from "KWANZAA: Everything You Always Wanted To Know But Didn't Know Where to Ask",
30th Anniversary Edition, by Cedric McClester. Published by Gumbs & Thomas Publishers, Inc. New York.

Other ways to practice the Nguzo Saba

Although Kwanzaa is observed for seven days, the Nguzo Saba and the spirit of the holiday can become part of our everyday lives. Listed below are ideas and suggestions for practicing the Nguzo Saba throughout the year.

- Give awards to family members who display self-discipline and determination in working toward or achieving a goal.
- Plan and attend family reunions.
- Explore the lives of your ancestors and share the information with other family members.
- Start a family educational fund.
- Open a savings account in a Black-owned bank.
- Patronize Black-owned businesses.
- Attend Black cultural exhibits, plays and concerts.
- Support Black artists by attending art shows and museums, and buying Black art for your home or office.
- Increase your knowledge of Black history by reading books, magazines and newspapers, and organize community reading clubs for young people.
- Enroll your children in a Rites of Passage program.
- Become a mentor to a young person.
- Volunteer to help your church, community school or social agency.

Kwanzaa Holiday Recipes

NO celebration would be complete without festive foods. In this section, we have compiled a variety of African, Caribbean, Brazilian, Creole and other dishes and beverages for your Karamu. Also included are two basic menu suggestions. Enjoy!

Spinach Salad
Ann Gamble, Temple Hills, MD

2 bags fresh spinach	1 small bag of radishes
1 small onion, thinly sliced	3 tbsps. bacon bits
1/2 cup cider vinegar	1/4 cup vegetable oil
Salt (optional)	

Remove stem from spinach. Discard. Tear spinach into small pieces. Wash 2 or 3 times in lukewarm water, and once in cold water. Shake off as much water as possible. Put spinach into plastic bag and refrigerate in crisper bin for about an hour. Wash radishes thoroughly, cutting off top and bottom. Cut into round thin slices. In large bowl, combine spinach, radish and onions. Mix thoroughly. In a tightly capped jar or bottle, shake together vinegar, oil, and salt. Just before serving, add oil and vinegar, and bacon bits. Toss lightly. Approx: 8 servings.

Ethiopian Lentil Salad*

2 1/2 cups (16 oz.) dry lentils	4 cloves garlic, minced
1 bottle (8 oz.) Kraft or Seven Seas	3 carrots, peeled, finely chopped
Red Wine Vinegar & Oil Dressing®	3 jalapeño peppers, seeded, minced

Place lentils in medium saucepan; fill with enough water to cover lentils by 2 inches. Cook on medium heat 25 to 30 minutes or until tender. (Do not overcook) Drain. Rinse with cold water. Drain thoroughly. Mix lentils with remaining ingredients. Refrigerate 2 hours or overnight. Stir before serving. Makes 8 servings.

*Reprinted with permission from Kraft Creative Kitchens.

Black-Eyed Pea Salad*
Joyce R. Broome, Washington, DC

2 (10 oz.) pkgs. frozen	1/2 cup chopped red pepper
black-eyed peas	1 bunch green onions, thinly sliced
1 cup Italian salad dressing	1/2 cup chopped green pepper
2 tsps. sugar	1/4 cup chopped parsley
1/4 tsp. crushed red pepper	salt and pepper to taste
1/2 cup sliced celery	lettuce leaves

Cook peas as directed on package; drain. Shake Italian dressing, sugar and crushed red pepper in tightly covered container. Combine cooked peas, dressing, celery, green and red peppers, onions, parsley, salt and pepper. Chill. Serve on lettuce leaves. Approx. 6 to 8 servings.

*Reprinted from "Sharing Our Best", J.U.G.S., Inc.

Crunchy Bacon Coleslaw*

3/4 cup Miracle Whip® or
   Miracle Whip Light Dressing®
5 cups shredded cabbage
4 slices Oscar Mayer® Bacon,
   crisply cooked, crumbled

1 tbsp. sugar
1/2 cup chopped peanuts
1 1/2 tsps. cider vinegar

Mix dressing and sugar in large bowl. Add remaining ingredients; mix lightly. Refrigerate. Makes 8 servings.

Reprinted with permission from Kraft Creative Kitchens.

Cabbage/Crab Salad
Inez Mallett, Manning, SC

1 large cabbage, shredded
1/2 cup green pepper, chopped
1 1/2 cups Miracle Whip® dressing
Salt & black pepper

1 cup carrots, shredded
1 large pkg. imitation crabmeat,
   lightly shredded

Select a firm cabbage, slightly green. No dark green leaves. In a large bowl, combine first four ingredients. Mix thoroughly. Add Miracle Whip®. Mix lightly. Season to taste with salt and pepper. Approx. 8 servings.

Potato Salad
Ida Gamble-Gumbs, New York, NY

5 lbs. all-purpose white potatoes
5 hard boiled eggs, chopped
1/2 small onion, chopped
2 tsps. celery seeds
1 tbsp. vinegar
Salt and black pepper

2 cups Miracle Whip® dressing
1 med. green pepper, diced
1/2 cup sweet relish
2 tsps prepared mustard
1 tsp. sugar (optional)
Paprika (optional)

Wash and scrub potatoes to remove any dirt or grit. Boil potatoes in skin until fully cooked but firm. Remove from water and set aside to cool. In a large mixing bowl, combine peeled-diced potatoes, celery seeds and black pepper. Lift lightly with fork to mix. Add onions, relish, egg and green pepper. Mix. In a small bowl, mix together Miracle Whip®, vinegar, mustard and sugar. Add to large bowl with potatoes and mix well. Season with salt and additional pepper if desired. Garnish with paprika. Approx. 12 servings.

String Beans with Potatoes
Francine McGill, Brooklyn, NY

3 lbs. fresh crisp string beans
1 pkg. smoked turkey
1 tsp. sugar

4 medium all-purpose white potatoes
Lawry's® seasoned salt
Black pepper

Wash turkey and boil in medium pot until tender. Remove ends and strings (if any) from beans. Wash thoroughly. Add to pot with turkey. Cover and cook for approx. 20 minutes. Meanwhile clean and peel potatoes. Cut into quarters and add to pot. Add sugar. Season to taste with seasoned salt and pepper. Cook until potatoes are tender, but not mushy. Approx. 8 servings.

Spicy Meatless Greens
Ida Gamble-Gumbs, New York, NY

4 lbs. fresh greens (collard, mustard, turnip greens, kale, etc.)
Goya® Jamón concentrate (ham flavored seasoning)

1 tbsp. crushed red pepper
2 tsps. sugar
3 tbsps. vegetable oil

Purchase fresh crisp greens. Remóve any large stems. Discard. Clean greens thoroughly by washing in several changes of water. In medium size pot, bring to a boil about 1/2 inch of water. Add greens. Cook uncovered for 5 minutes. Cover and cook until tender. Do not overcook. Add remaining ingredients and simmer for about 3 minutes. Remove from heat and let stand for about 20 minutes before serving. Approx. 8 to 10 servings.

Scalloped Vegetables

1 large bag mixed vegetables, frozen
1 cup mayonnaise
1 med. onion, grated
1 box crackers (Ritz®, Townhouse®, etc.) crushed fine

1 cup cheddar cheese, grated
1 stick butter, melted
1 cup celery, chopped
1/2 tsp. salt (optional)

Cook vegetables for about 5 minutes in 1/2 cup of slightly salted water. Drain water from vegetables and place into a 2 qt. casserole. Mix together onion, celery, cheese, and mayonnaise. Spoon onto top of vegetables. Combine cracker crumbs with butter and sprinkle on top of mixture. Bake at 350 degrees until vegetables are cooked and crumbs are brown. Approx. 6 servings.

Fried Plantains

6 Yellow plantains
Palm or olive oil for frying

Cinnamon or cayenne pepper (optional)

Rinse unpeeled plantains in lukewarm water. Peel. Save skin. Cut plantains in half. Slice. Fry in hot oil until golden brown. Sprinkle with cinnamon or cayenne pepper. Cover with plantain skin until ready to serve. Approx. 8 servings.

Stringbean Patties
Warren Barksdale, New York, NY

1 16 oz. can French-style string beans, drained
3/4 - 1 cup grated cheese
1 - 2 cloves of garlic, minced
1 tsp. salsa (optional)
Salt & pepper to taste

1 egg
1 can mushrooms, drained (stems and pieces) (optional)
1/2 chopped onion (optional)
1/2 - 3/4 cup bread crumbs
Vegetable oil for frying

Mix all ingredients. Add enough bread crumbs to hold mixture together. Form into patties. Heat oil in skillet, and add patties. Fry on one side until set. Note: If patties are turned too soon, they will fall apart. Turn over when brown. Fry until golden and somewhat firm. Approx. 6 to 8 servings.

Fried Okra
Warren Barksdale, New York, NY

1 lb. okra
1 cup flour
Oil for frying

1 cup corn meal
Salt & pepper

Wash okra and cut into pieces. Salt and pepper to taste. Mix corn meal and flour. Heat oil in skillet. Coat okra with meal and flour mixture. Shake off excess. Fry in oil until golden brown. Approx. 6 to 8 servings.

Stuffed Mushrooms
Harold Thomas, New York, NY

2 lbs. mushrooms (Stems removed and chopped fine)
1 large onion (minced)
2 stalks celery (minced)
1/2 stick butter or margarine

1 large green pepper (minced)
3 cloves garlic (minced)
Bread crumbs
Seasoning to taste

Preheat oven to 375 degrees. Bake mushroom caps for 5 minutes. Remove and let cool. In large saucepan, sauté onions, peppers, garlic and celery in 2 tablespoons of butter for about 4 minutes. Add more butter as needed. Add seasonings and mushroom stems to mixture and cook for 3 minutes more. Stir constantly to prevent burning. As mixture is simmering, add bread crumbs until texture of stuffing. Cook for few more minutes. Stuff mushroom caps. Arrange on baking sheet and bake for 10 minutes. Approx. 10 to 12 servings.

Black Beans
Beverly Green, Flushing, NY

Bag (1 lb.) black beans	10 cups of water
1 large green pepper, diced	1 large onion
4 cloves of garlic, diced	1 bay leaf
2/3 cup olive oil	4 tsps. of salt
1/2 tsp. of black pepper	1/4 tsp. oregano
2 tbsps. vinegar	2 tbsps. sugar
2 tbsps. cooking wine	

Wash beans thoroughly. Place beans and water in large pot 1 - 2 hours before cooking. Once beans have swollen, place pot over heat and bring to a boil. Add remaining ingredients. Cover pot and simmer until beans are soft. With a fork, mash a few beans in the pot. If there is too much liquid in pot, simmer uncovered for a few minutes. Remove bay leaf and serve. Approx 10 to 12 servings.

Stir Fry Turkey*
Louis Bailey, Executive Chef, Air Jamaica

8 oz. Turkey Breast	4 tbsps. Pickapeppa™ Sauce
2 tbsps. Soy Sauce	1 tbsp. Cornstarch
4 oz. Carrots (Julienne)	4 oz. Onions (Julienne)
4 oz. Zucchini (Julienne)	3-4 tbsps. Oil
Seasoning	

Combine Pickapeppa™ sauce and soy sauce to make a marinade. Cut turkey into long strips. Marinate turkey strips in the sauce for 15-20 minutes. Heat wok or skillet - add oil to wok or skillet. Remove turkey from marinade and stir fry. Add julienne of vegetables to the turkey. Combine cornstarch and marinade and stir into the turkey and vegetables. Cook for a few minutes. Serve hot.

Reprinted with permission from Air Jamaica.

Creole Chicken*

2 tbsps. olive oil	1 1/2 to 3 lbs. broiler-fryer chicken, cut up
2 medium onions, sliced	
2 cloves garlic, minced	1 16-ounce can stewed tomatoes
1 green pepper, chopped	1 tbsp. gumbo file
1 8-ounce can tomato sauce	1/4 tsp. cayenne pepper
1 tsp. dried thyme	Salt to taste
1 10-ounce package frozen sliced okra	Cooked yellow rice or white rice

Heat olive oil in 12-inch skillet until hot. Cook chicken over medium heat until brown on all sides, about 15 minutes. Drain drippings from skillet. Stir in remaining ingredients except okra and rice. Heat to boiling, reduce heat. Cover and simmer for 30 minutes. Stir in okra. Heat to boiling. Reduce heat. Cover and simmer until thickest pieces of chicken are done and okra is tender, about 10 minutes. Serve with rice.

Reprinted with permission from Amalgamated Publishers, Inc.

Fried Buttermilk Chicken
Catherine Stephens, Manning, SC

4 lbs. chicken parts	3 cups buttermilk
2 cups self-rising flour	1 cup bread crumbs
2 tbsps. garlic powder	2 tbsps. onion powder
2 tbsps. poultry seasoning	1 tbsp. paprika
Salt & black pepper	Oil for deep frying

Clean chicken thoroughly. Marinate in buttermilk for 3-4 hours. In a plastic bag, combine dry ingredients. Add salt and pepper to taste. Shake well. Remove chicken from buttermilk, shaking off any excess. Drop a few pieces of chicken at a time into plastic bag. Shake to coat. Place coated chicken on aluminum foil and let stand for approx 30 minutes. Meanwhile, in a large pot, heat oil until sizzling. Place a few pieces of chicken in pot and cook until golden brown and tender, approx. 15 minutes. Serves 12.

Jamaican Jerk Chicken
Beverly Smith, New York, NY

4 lbs. chicken parts	2 tbsps. onion powder
2 tbsps. garlic powder	1 med. onion, chopped
1 clove garlic, minced	1 cup chopped scallions
1 tsp. Walker's Wood jerk seasoning*	1 tbsp. Fachoy soy sauce*

Clean chicken thoroughly. Place in large bowl (do not use plastic bowl). Mix other ingredients together with chicken, and marinate overnight in refrigerator. The amount of jerk seasoning may be increased if desired. Next day, preheat oven to 350 degrees. Place chicken on rack in roasting pan. Use marinade from bowl to baste chicken while cooking. With basting brush, baste chicken on both sides. Continue this process until chicken is done. Approx. 10 servings.

*Other brands of jerk seasoning and soy sauce may be used if necessary.

Deep Fried Barbecue-Flavored Chicken
Ida Gamble-Gumbs, New York, NY

3 lbs. chicken parts	1 bottle barbecue sauce
1 tbsp. pepper sauce or hot sauce (optional)	2 tbsps. prepared mustard
2 tbsps. vinegar	1 tbsp. sugar
salt and pepper	Garlic powder
3 cups self-rising flour	Oil for deep frying

Clean chicken thoroughly. In large pot, parboil chicken parts for 20 minutes. While chicken is boiling, combine barbecue sauce, hot sauce, mustard, vinegar and sugar. Bring to a boil over medium heat, stirring constantly. Remove from heat and let cool. Drain water from chicken, let chicken cool. Marinate chicken in barbecue sauce mixture in refrigerator, 3 to 4 hours or overnight. On a sheet of aluminum foil, mix flour with desired amounts of garlic powder, salt and pepper. Shake off excess barbecue sauce from chicken. Roll chicken in flour mixture and drop into hot oil. Deep fry until golden brown. Drain on paper towels. Approx. 8 servings.

African Peanut Butter Chicken

4 lbs. chicken parts, cleaned
2 large onions, sliced
1 large red pepper, cut in strips   1/4 cup tomato paste
1/2 tsp. cayenne pepper   1/2 cup peanut butter
1 tsp. curry powder   2 tsps. salt

Bake chicken in uncovered roasting pan at 350 degrees about 45 minutes. Chicken should be a nice brown. Remove chicken from pan. Pour drippings from roasting pan into a medium size saucepan. Return chicken to roasting pan, set aside. Stir salt, cayenne pepper and curry powder into drippings in saucepan. Cook for 1 minute. Add onions and red pepper. Cook for 3 minutes. Meanwhile, thin tomato paste with about 1/2 cup water. Add to vegetables in saucepan and simmer for about 5 minutes. While mixture in saucepan is cooking, thin peanut butter with about 2 tbsps. of water. Add to saucepan. Pour over chicken in roasting pan. Cover pan with top or aluminum foil. Return to oven and bake for about 15 minutes. Serve with rice. Approx. 10 servings.

Kwanzaa's Bahian Shrimp*

1 lb. medium shrimp
1/2 cup heavy cream   1/2 cup cooking oil
1 tsp. chopped parsley   1 tbsp. shredded coconut

Sauté shrimp in olive oil. Add cooking wine, coconut and cream. Simmer for 5 minutes. Sprinkle with parsley.

* *Reprinted with permission from Amalgamated Publishers, Inc.*

Crisp Fried Scallops With Spinach Dip
Ernie Wyatt, New York, NY

Scallops

1/2 cup all-purpose flour
1 cup plain yogurt
1/4 cup mayonnaise
1/3 cup scallions, chopped
2 cups fine dry bread crumbs
2 lbs. bay scallops
Corn oil for deep frying
Lemon wedges

Spinach dip

3/4 pound spinach
2 large eggs
1/2 tsp. salt & 1/4 tsp. cayenne pepper
  or to taste
1/4 tsp. minced tarragon
2 cloves of garlic
1 tsp. white wine vinegar or or taste

In 3 separate bowls, have ready the flour, eggs beaten with the salt and cayenne pepper, and the bread crumbs. Toss scallops in flour, coating them thoroughly. Place in colander and shake off any excess flour. Add scallops to egg mixture, coating them and transfer to bread crumbs, letting excess egg drip off. Toss scallops with bread crumbs, transferring them as they are coated to a sheet of wax paper. In a Dutch oven pot, heat 1 inch of oil until it registers 350 degrees on a deep fat thermometer. Drop scallops in hot oil by handfuls, fry for 1 minute, or until crisp. Transfer scallops with a slotted spoon to paper towels to drain. Serve scallops, spinach dip and lemon wedges.

cont'd

Dip:

Discard coarse stems from spinach, wash leaves well and drain. In a large heavy saucepan, cook spinach in salted water, covered, over moderate heat for 3 to 4 minutes or until wilted. Refresh in a bowl of ice cubes and cold water. In a colander, drain well. With hands, squeeze spinach dry and place in a blender. Add yogurt, mayonnaise, scallions, garlic, tarragon, vinegar, salt and pepper to taste, and puree.

Congo Fish / American Version*

1 tbsp. butter
1 cup onion, chopped
1/4 tsp. black pepper
1 lb. greens (collards, kale, spinach, etc.)
Cayenne pepper and salt to taste

1 tbsp. peanut oil
1/2 cup green pepper, chopped
2 cups water
1 lb. frozen fish fillets, slightly thawed

Sauté the onion and green pepper in the fat. When soft, add water, greens, and fish cut into chunks. Cover, cooking until tender. (Add more water if necessary.) Season to taste. Serve over fufu or rice.

Reprinted from "Soul on Rice", by Patricia B. Mitchell.

Spicy Oven-Fried Catfish*

4 dressed catfish, about 7 ounces each
1/4 cup dry bread crumbs
1/2 tsp. paprika
1/8 tsp. cayenne pepper
1/2 cup skim milk

1/4 cup yellow cornmeal
1/2 tsp. salt
1/2 tsp. garlic powder
1/8 tsp. ground thyme
1/4 cup margarine, melted

Heat oven to 450 degrees. Combine cornmeal, bread crumbs, salt, paprika, garlic powder, cayenne pepper and thyme. Dip fish into milk. Coat with cornmeal mixture. Place in 12 x 9 x 2-inch rectangular pan, coated with vegetable cooking spray. Pour margarine over fish. Bake uncovered until fish flakes very easily with fork, about 15 to 20 minutes.

* *Reprinted with permission from Amalgamated Publishers, Inc.*

Stuffed Bluefish
Ida Gamble-Gumbs, New York, NY

4 - 5 lb. bluefish	2 1/2 cups seasoned bread crumbs
1/2 stick margarine	1/2 cup chopped onion
1/2 cup chopped green pepper	Salt & black pepper to taste
Bacon (6 strips)	

Purchase 4-5 lb. whole fish with backbone removed. Clean thoroughly. Rub oil on outside of fish, and season lightly inside and out with salt and pepper. Set aside. In a saucepan, melt margarine. Sauté onion and green pepper for 2 minutes over low heat. Add bread crumbs and mix thoroughly adding about two tablespoons of water if necessary. Bread crumbs should not be too moist. (The fish will generate enough moisture for the stuffing) In a shallow baking pan, line bacon horizontally. Lay opened fish on bacon and spoon bread crumb mixture onto one side. Fold other side of fish over side with bread crumbs. Wrap strips of bacon around stuffed fish and bake uncovered until fish is done. Approx. 45 minutes. Fish should be crisp on the outside. Approx. 6 servings.

Catfish Stew
Ernie Wyatt, New York, NY

1 to 2 lb package of bacon	1 1/2 cups finely chopped onions
4 to 5 lbs. catfish fillets, cut into 1 1/2 inch pieces	2 lbs. catfish trimmings: head, tail, and bones
6 large boiling potatoes, peeled and cut into cubes	10 med. sized firm, ripe tomatoes, washed, cored and cut into 1/1/2 inch pieces
Freshly ground black pepper	
Worcestershire sauce	Tabasco® sauce
Salt	Cheese cloth

In a large cast iron pot, fry bacon over moderate heat, turning until crisp and brown and all fat rendered. Transfer to paper towels, drain and cool, then crumble into small bits and set aside. Remove half of fat from pot and add onions, stirring frequently. Cook over moderate heat for about 8 minutes or until onions are caramelized and soft but not brown. Stir in the tomatoes and potatoes. Place catfish trimmings in cheese cloth, add to pot and simmer for about 1 1/2 hours on a very low flame. Remove the cheese cloth with trimmings and add Worcestershire sauce, tabasco®, salt and pepper to taste. Add the catfish fillets and reserved bacon. Mix well. Cover pot tightly and continue to simmer over low heat until fish flakes easily when prodded gently with a fork. Taste for seasoning and serve. Approx. 8 servings.

Oxtails with Kidney Beans
Noill Martin, Palm Bay, FL.

2 - 3 lbs. Oxtails
1 tsp. curry powder
2 stalks celery, diced
Sugar
1 16 oz. can kidney beans

1 med. green pepper, chopped
1 large onion, chopped
Oil
Salt & pepper to taste

Wash oxtails. Dry. Season with salt, pepper, and curry powder. In saucepan, heat oil. Add a small amount of sugar for browning. Brown oxtails. Remove from saucepan. Cut up vegetables and put in pressure cooker: Put oxtails on top of vegetables. Add 2 cups of water. Rocker on top of pressure cooker should rock for 30 minutes. Let pressure drop of its own accord. Add 1 can kidney beans to mixture. Heat thoroughly. Serve with rice. Approx. 6 - 8 servings.

African Jollof Rice

1 3 or 4 lb. chicken
4 medium tomatoes
1/2 lb. shrimp
1/2 bag (16 oz.) frozen peas and carrots
1 tsp. black pepper
1 tsp. dried thyme
Goya® Sazon for coloring

6 medium onions, chopped
4 green bell peppers, chopped
1 1/2 cups chopped boiled ham
1 tsp. salt
1/2 tsp. cayenne pepper
5 cups cooked dry rice

Clean chicken thoroughly. Chop into small pieces, removing as many of the bones as possible. In a large cast iron pot, brown chicken in small amount of oil. Add onions and green peppers. Sauté over medium heat for 5 minutes. Meanwhile in a separate saucepan, sauté shrimp in small amount of oil until pink. Add shrimp, ham, tomatoes, salt, pepper and thyme to chicken. Let simmer for about 15 minutes. Add peas and carrots. When chicken is tender, add mixture to rice and serve. Sazon® may be added for coloring. Serves 10.

West Indian Peas and Rice
Beverly Smith, New York, NY

Dry or canned pigeon peas	Coconut milk
1 cup scallions	Butter or margarine
Uncle Ben's® rice - 2 cups	Thyme

Dry Peas - 1 cup

Pick out any bad peas or rocks. Wash thoroughly. Soak in 3 cups of water until swollen. Bring peas to a boil in same water. Reduce heat to low and boil for about 30 minutes, Add 1 cup of coconut milk, 1/2 teaspoon thyme, 1 cup scallions, 2 cups rice, 2 tablespoons butter or margarine, and salt if desired. Cook very slowly until rice is fluffy. A little water can be added during cooking if necessary. Lift lightly with fork to mix peas and rice together. Approx. 8 servings.

Canned Peas - 14 oz.

Empty entire contents of can into a medium pot. Add 1 can of water, 1/3 can of coconut milk and all other ingredients as shown above. Cook over very low heat until rice is fluffy.

Chicken Pilaf Rice
Dorothy Gamble, Manning, SC

5 cups long grain rice	8 cups homemade chicken broth
3 lbs. chicken backs	1 lb. chicken thighs
Instant or granulated chicken bouillon	Salt and black pepper

Broth

Clean chicken thoroughly. In a large pot, combine water (use enough water to yield 8 cups of broth), chicken and 2 tsps. each salt and pepper. Simmer covered until chicken is tender. Remove chicken from broth. Remove skin and bones from chicken. Discard. Shred chicken into small pieces and place in bowl. Spoon a small amount of broth on chicken and set aside. Strain broth. Return strained broth to pot. Let cool until fat is settled on top. Remove most of fat, but not all.

Rice

In same pot, season to taste the broth with instant or granulated bouillon. Bring to boil. Add rice and bring to second boil. Reduce heat to low and simmer covered until rice is cooked. Halfway through cooking, fluff rice with fork. Remove rice from heat when cooked, set aside to cool. In a large pot, make layers, alternating shredded chicken and rice. Use only a small amount of chicken for layers. Reheat if necessary when ready to serve. Serves 15.

Stir-Fried Mushroom Rice
Inez G. Mallett, Manning, SC

4 cups cooked rice	1 pkg. fresh mushrooms
2 tbsps. veg. cooking oil	1 pkg. oriental stir-fry rice seasoning mix
2 tbsps. soy sauce	Garlic and parsley seasoning

Follow instructions on package for cooking rice. Do not add salt. Rice should be as dry as possible. Let cooked rice stand in refrigerator 3-4 hours or overnight. Wash and slice mushrooms, completely draining all excess water. Using one tablespoon of cooking oil, stir-fry rice with oriental seasoning in wok or large frying pan. Heat one tablespoon of cooking oil in small frying pan. Add mushrooms and stir-fry for about one minute. Sprinkle garlic parsley seasoning over mushrooms while cooking. Add to rice. Mix thoroughly so that mushrooms will be distributed evenly throughout rice. Season to taste with soy sauce. Let stand for about 30 minutes or more before serving. Approx 8 - 10 servings.

Caribbean Red Beans and Rice
Cynthia Weathers, Bronx, NY

3/4 bag (16 oz.) red beans	4 cups extra long grain rice
1 cup chopped onions	1/2 cup chopped celery
2 lbs. smoked neckbones	Salt and pepper to taste

Rinse beans thoroughly. Cover with water in medium bowl and soak until beans are swollen. Combine beans with smoked meat and cook until both are tender. Add celery and onions halfway through cooking. Remove bones from meat, and leave a portion of the meat in pot. There should be enough liquid in pot to yield 5 cups. Season to taste with salt and pepper. Add rice. Bring to a boil. Reduce heat to low and cook very slowly until rice is nice and fluffy. It may be necessary to sprinkle with a little water from time to time. Remove from heat and serve. Approx. 12 servings.

Hoppin John
Martha Gamble, Brooklyn, NY

2 cups dried cow or field peas	2 quarts water
1 pkg. smoked ham hocks or neckbones*	2 tsps. salt (optional)
3 cups uncooked extra long grain rice	1 tsp. sugar (optional)

Pick out any bad peas and rocks. Wash thoroughly. Cover peas with cold water and soak until swollen. Meanwhile, boil meat over medium heat approximately 1 hour. Add drained peas, sugar, and salt. Cook for approximately 30 minutes. Remove meat from bones. Discard fat meat and skin. Shred lean meat slightly and return to pot. There should be enough liquid in pot to yield about 4 cups. Add rice and boil covered, over very low heat until rice is cooked. Lift lightly to mix. Remove peas and rice mixture to a serving dish. Serve immediately. Mixture should be firm, not dry or mushy. Approx. 8 - 10 servings.

*Smoked turkey may be substituted for pork.

Macaroni and Cheese with Pimentos
Betty Gilmore, Jamaica, NY

1 8-oz. box elbow macaroni
1 8-oz. jar Cheeze Whiz®
5 eggs
1 stick butter or margarine
Black pepper to taste

12 oz. American cheese, slices
16 oz. sharp cheddar cheese, grated
1 1/2 cup milk, or more
1 small jar pimentos, chopped
1 tbsp. cooking oil

Boil macaroni in slightly salted water (salt optional) with 1 tablespoon of cooking oil. Meanwhile cut up American cheese, reserving 3 or 4 slices. Drain water from cooked macaroni, and add butter or margarine, Cheese Whiz®, cheddar, and cut up American cheese. Mix thoroughly. Add milk. Beat eggs slightly, and add to macaroni mixture. Mix. Add pimentos and black pepper. Pour into baking pan, and bake in pre-heated oven (375 degrees) until cooked. Place reserved slices of cheese on top of mixture about 15 minutes before removing from oven. Approx. 10 - 12 servings.

Hot Cheese Biscuits
Ida Gamble-Gumbs, New York, NY

2 cups self-rising flour
About 2/3 - 3/4 cup buttermilk

1/2 cup shortening
1 cup cheddar cheese, shredded

Preheat oven to 425 degrees. In medium bowl, add flour. With fork, work shortening into flour. Mixture should be like coarse corn meal. Add cheese, mixing lightly. Pour in half of milk, mix lightly with fork. Add enough milk to make dough moist enough to leave side of bowl. Turn dough onto lightly floured surface. Knead gently about 5 or 6 times. With rolling pin, lightly roll dough out from center. Roll about 1/2 inch thick. With biscuit cutter, cut out biscuits. Place onto ungreased cookie sheet. Brush top of biscuits with melted butter. Bake 12 to 15 minutes or until nicely browned. Yields approx. 12.

Spicy Cornbread*

1/2 cup Miracle Whip® or
    Miracle Whip Light Dressing®
2 eggs, beaten
1 can (11 oz.) whole kernel corn, drained
1/2 cup chopped red bell pepper

1 can (4 oz.) chopped green chilies,
    undrained
1/2 tsp. ground red pepper
2 pkg. (8-1/2 oz. each) corn muffin mix

Mix dressing, chilies, eggs and ground red pepper in large bowl. Add remaining ingredients; mix just until moistened. Pour into greased 13 x 9-inch baking pan. Bake at 400 degrees F for 25 to 30 minutes or until golden brown. Approx 12 servings. *Variation:* Spicy cornbread muffins: Spoon batter into paper-lined muffin pans. Bake at 400 degrees F for 15 to 20 minutes. Makes 24 muffins.

Reprinted with permission from Kraft Creative Kitchens.

Carolina Rolls
Betty Gilmore, Jamaica, NY

6 1/2 cups all-purpose flour
1 cup buttermilk
1/4 cup sugar, or to taste
1/3 cup whole milk, scalded
2 tbsps. melted butter

3 pkgs. active dry yeast
1 cup Crisco®
2 eggs, beaten
2 tsps. salt

Cool scalded milk to lukewarm. Add yeast and let dissolve. In large bowl, sift flour and add dry ingredients. Mix Crisco® into flour mixture, and work together. Add scalded milk with yeast and buttermilk to flour. Add egg, and stir until blended to form stiff dough. Separate dough into two balls and place into large greased bowls, turning dough to grease well. Cover with wax paper and clean towel and let rise in warm place until double in size. Turn dough onto floured surface, knead until smooth and elastic. Cut off pieces of dough, and form into 2" balls. Place in baking pan, allowing balls to slightly touch each other. Cover and let rise again. Brush top with melted butter or margarine and bake at 400 degrees until brown. Yields approx 3 dz.

Old-Fashioned Teacakes

Self-rising flour
3/4 cup sugar, or more
1 tbsp. lemon or vanilla extract
1/2 tsp. nutmeg

1 stick butter
1/3 cup canned milk
2 large eggs, beaten

Cream together butter and sugar. Add eggs and cream thoroughly. Sift together 2 cups of flour and nutmeg. Stir into creamed mixture. Add milk and blend thoroughly. Add additional flour, if necessary, to make dough firm enough to roll. Form into ball and refrigerate for 1 or 2 hours. Roll dough 1/4 inch thick on a floured surface. Cut into 2 1/2 inch squares. Place on greased baking sheet, slightly touching each other, and bake at 350 degrees for about 15 minutes. Yields approx. 1 dz.

Sweet Potato Pie
Ida Gamble-Gumbs, New York, NY

3 to 4 medium sweet potatoes
3/4 stick of butter
1 tbsp. pure lemon flavor
Pinch of salt

1 cup sugar
1 tbsp. nutmeg
1 egg
2 9-inch pie crusts*

Let butter stand at room temperature until soft. Clean potatoes and boil in skin until fully cooked. Remove cooked potatoes from water and let stand at room temperature until cool enough to peel. Pre-heat oven to 325 degrees. In medium bowl, mash potatoes with masher or fork for about 30 seconds. Add sugar and butter, mix with electric mixer until smooth. Blend in egg. Add remaining ingredients and mix well. Divide evenly into pie crusts and bake until potato filling is set, and crust is golden brown, approximately 30 minutes. Cool and serve.

*Certain pie crusts may require browning before filling. Follow directions on package.

Walnut Pound Cake
Ida Gamble-Gumbs, New York, NY

1 lb. of butter	3 cups cake flour
1-16 oz. box confectioners sugar	6 eggs
1 1/2 cups chopped walnuts	1/4 cup flour
1 tbsp. pure vanilla flavor	1 tbsp. pure lemon flavor

Cream together butter and sugar. Add eggs, one at a time. Mix for approximately three minutes. To creamed mixture, add three cups of flour. Mix thoroughly after each cup. On a sheet of wax paper or aluminum foil, dust walnuts in remaining flour. Shake off excess flour. Add walnuts to mixture. Bake in a greased cake pan for approximately 1 hour and 20 minutes, 325 degrees F. NOTE: Do not pre-heat oven.

Jelly Layer Cake
Essie Gamble, Manning, SC

3 cups self-rising cake flour	1 1/2 cups granulated sugar
1 1/2 sticks of butter	1 heaping tbsp. shortening
3/4 cup whole milk	1/4 cup ice cold water
2 tbsps. pure lemon flavor	1 1/2 cups apple jelly*
3 eggs	1/2 tsp. lemon flavor

Let eggs, butter and shortening stand at room temperature approximately 2 hours. Preheat oven to 325 degrees. In large bowl, combine butter, shortening and sugar. Using electric mixer, set on high speed, mix for about 3 minutes. Add eggs, one at a time, beating thoroughly after each egg. Mix until light and fluffy. At low speed, gradually add in alternately flour and milk, then 2 tbsps. lemon flavor. Mix until smooth. Divide evenly into four 9-inch cake pans. (Pan should be greased with shortening and dusted lightly with flour.) Bake on two racks. Do not place one pan directly over the other. Bake for about 30 minutes, or until golden brown and toothpick inserted in center comes out clean. Let stand for about 20 minutes.

In small bowl, combine jelly with 1/2 tsp. lemon flavor. Beat with hand beater or fork for about 30 seconds. Spread evenly on three layers. First three layers should be upside down, fourth layer top side up. Do not spread jelly on top layer.

* Your favorite jelly or jam may be substituted for apple jelly.

Sweet Potato Layer Cake

2 1/2 cups sifted cake flour
2 cups sugar
1 1/2 cup raw sweet potatoes, grated
4 eggs
4 Tbsps. hot water
1 cup chopped walnuts or pecans
1/4 tsp. salt

1 tsp. cinnamon
1 tsp. nutmeg
1 tsp. vanilla flavor
1 1/2 cup cooking oil
3 9-inch cake pans
3 tsps. baking powder

Mix together flour, baking powder, salt, cinnamon, nutmeg, and vanilla. Set aside. Combine oil, sugar, and eggs with hot water. Add flour and mix. Stir in sweet potatoes and nuts. Mix thoroughly. Turn into three 9-inch cake pans and bake at 350 degrees for about thirty minutes. Let cool before frosting.

Frosting

1 box confectioners sugar
1 tsp. vanilla flavor
can milk (optional)

1 8-oz. pkg. cream cheese
1 pkg. flaked coconut

With electric mixer, gradually mix confectioners sugar with cream cheese. Add milk, if necessary. Stir in vanilla. Mix well. Fill and frost cake layers. Sprinkle with coconut.

Pinto Bean Cake[*]

1 cup sugar
2 tsps. vanilla
2 cups cooked unseasoned pinto beans, mashed
1 tsp. baking soda
1 tsp. cinnamon
1/2 cup nuts, chopped

1 stick butter or margarine
2 eggs
1 cup flour
1/2 tsp. salt
1 tsp. allspice or 1/2 tsp. cloves
1 cup raisins
2 cups finely chopped peeled apples

Cream sugar and butter or margarine; add vanilla and eggs. Beat in well-mashed beans; stir in dry ingredients, then add nuts, raisins, and apples. Bake in a greased and floured tube pan for 1 hour at 325 degrees F.

[*]Reprinted from "Soul on Rice" by Patricia B. Mitchell.

Peach Cobbler with Nutmeg Crust
Hazel Parker, Bronx, NY

Crust
3 cups all-purpose flour	1/2 cup sugar
1 tsp. nutmeg	1/2 stick of chilled butter
1/2 cup shortening	Ice cold water (approx. 1/3 cup)
1/2 tsp. salt	

Filling

3/4 stick butter	1 cup sugar
1 tsp. cinnamon	1/2 tsp. nutmeg
1 tbsp. vanilla flavor	1 tbsp. flour
2 tbsps. water	8 large peaches

Dough for Crust

In large bowl, blend together flour, sugar, salt and nutmeg. Cut butter and shortening into flour mixture. Mix until crumbly. Add water, a little at a time to make dough. Cut into two parts and form into balls. Wrap in wax paper and place in refrigerator for one hour. Roll out one ball of dough for bottom crust and place into bottom of baking dish. Form dough trimmings into a ball. Roll out and cut into strips to be used as a layer between the filling.

To make cobbler, wash and peel peaches and cut into 1/2 inch slices. In saucepan, combine peaches, butter, sugar, cinnamon, and nutmeg. Cook over medium heat for approx 5 min, stirring constantly. Add vanilla and remove from heat. In small bowl, mix together 1 tbsp. of flour and water. Add to peaches. Return to heat and cook, stirring constantly until mixture thickens. Remove from heat. Spoon 1/2 of peach mixture into baking dish. Place dough strips on top of peach mixture. Spoon balance of peach mixture onto strips of dough in baking dish. Roll out the other half of dough for top crust and place on top of peach mixture. With knife, make a few slits in top crust. Preheat oven to 350 degrees and bake for approx 45 minutes, or until golden brown. Remove from oven, sprinkle top with a little cinnamon and sugar. Return to oven for 4 or 5 minutes. Serve hot. Approx: 6 to 8 servings.

Paradise Punch*

1 envelope (2 qt. size) KOOL-AID® Orange flavor Sugar-Sweetened Soft Drink Mix	8 cups (2 qt.) pineapple-orange juice 1 tsp. rum extract (optional) 2 cups ice cubes

Place soft drink mix in large plastic or glass pitcher. Add juice and extract; stir to dissolve. Refrigerate. Stir in ice cubes just before serving. Makes 10 1-cup servings.

Reprinted with permission from Kraft Creative Kitchens.

Coconut Cream Punch
Ida Gamble-Gumbs, New York, NY

1 14-oz. can coconut milk	3 qts. cold milk
1 1/2 cup cold cream	2 1/2 cups sugar
2 tsps. lemon juice	1 tbsp. coconut extract
5 2-liter bottles ginger ale	Vanilla ice cream
Pinch of salt	Yellow food coloring

Combine coconut milk, cold milk, cold cream, sugar, lemon juice, extract, food coloring, and salt. Blend well. Pour into round plastic containers and freeze for 24 hours. About 45 minutes before serving, remove from plastic containers and place into large punch bowl. Pour desired amount of ginger ale over frozen mixture. Garnish with scoops of ice cream. Approx. 24 servings.

Hot Kwanzaa Punch

1 qt. apple juice	3 oranges
1 qt. tea, sweetened	1 qt. orange juice
1 qt. pineapple juice	1 qt. cranberry juice
2 cups whole cranberry sauce	1 tsp. cloves
6 sticks cinnamon	Juice of 1 lemon

Slice oranges into wedges, then into tiny pieces. Place all ingredients into a pot and boil for about 10 minutes. Serve hot. Sugar may be added if desired. Yields 12 to 15 servings.

Suggested Menus

MENU #1

Black-Eyed Pea Salad
African Peanut Butter Chicken
Yellow or White Rice
Spicy Meatless Greens
Hot Cheese Biscuits
Peach Cobbler with Nutmeg Crust
Coconut Cream Punch

MENU #2

Spinach Salad
Spicy Oven-Fried Catfish
West Indian Peas and Rice
Crunchy Bacon Coleslaw
Fried Plantains
Spicy Cornbread
Jelly Layer Cake
Paradise Punch

African Fashion Ideas

DURING the 1960's, an increasing number of African-Americans began to wear African-style clothing as an expression of their new identity with Africa and African culture. Today many people wear traditional African attire when attending Kwanzaa celebrations.

In this section, we have included several African fashion designs for men and women, along with step-by-step information on the art of African headwrapping for women.

Nigerian Fabrics & Fashions,
New York

Fatou's Fashion Designs,
New York

Fatou's Fashion Designs,
New York

Nigerian Fabrics & Fashions,
New York

NOTE: See "Shopper's Guide" for complete address.

The Art of Headwrapping

One of the easiest Afrocentric items that can be worn during the Kwanzaa celebration is the Gele. Below are instructions on the African art of headwrapping.

Step 1. Use a two yard length of fabric 45" wide. The two raw ends of the gele can be folded and machine hemmed if desired. Fold the length of the gele as indicated.

Step 2. Begin the wrap on the left side of your head, with the short ends facing the back of the head.

Step 3. While holding the beginning portion securely, wrap the length around (low on the forehead) and toward the back. Continue wrapping around the back and up the left side, overlapping where you began.

Step 4. As you approach the center front of the forehead, the fabric should form an inverted V.

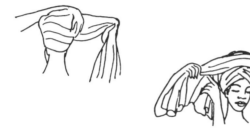

Steps 5, 6, 7. Continue to wrap as illustrated.

Step 8. The tail of the wrap should be brought around the side or back of the head and tucked securely between the folds.

Kwanzaa Glossary

Asante (Ah-SAHN-tay) - Swahili phrase for thank you.

Bendera (Bayn-DEH-rah) - National Black Liberation flag, created by Black nationalist Marcus Garvey and bearing the colors red, black and green. Black represents the people, red the struggle we have endured, and green, hope in the future.

Habari Gani? (Hah-bah-ree GAH-nee) - Swahili phrase meaning "what's the news?" and the opening statement each night of the Kwanzaa ceremony.

Harambee! Hah-RAHM-bay) - Swahili phrase invoking unity. Often it is said in sets of seven as a reinforcement of the principles of Kwanzaa.

Heri Za Kwanzaa (Hay ree zah KWAHN-zah) - Happy Kwanzaa.

Imani (Ee-MAH-nee) - One of the seven principles of Kwanzaa meaning faith and celebrated on the last day of Kwanzaa.

Karamu (Kah-RAH-moo) - a lavish feast and cultural celebration held on the eve before Kwanzaa's end.

Kikombe Cha Umoja (Kee-KOM-beh Cha Oo-MOH-jah) - unity cup used for the libation salute to the ancestors and to posterity.

Kinara (Kee-NAH-rah) - The Kwanzaa candle holder.

Kujichagulia (Koo-jee-chah-goo-LEE-ah) - One of the seven principles of Kwanzaa meaning self-determination and celebrated on the second day of the holiday.

Kuumba (Koo-OOM-bah) - One of the seven principles of Kwanzaa meaning creativity and celebrated on the sixth day of the holiday.

Kwanzaa (KWAHN-zah) - The African-American cultural celebration created by Dr. Maulana Karenga to help instill pride in one's cultural heritage.

Mazao (MAH-ZAH-oh) - Usually represented by a bowl of fruits, vegetables and nuts which rests on the mkeka, and represents the fruits of the harvest.

Mishumaa Saba (Mee-Shoo-MAH SAH-bah) - The seven candles of Kwanzaa -- one black, three red and three green. Each candle corresponds to one of the seven principles.

Mkeka (Em-KAY-kah) - Mat, either straw or cloth, used in the Kwanzaa ceremony and representing the African tradition.

Muhindi (Moo-HEEN-dee) - The ear or ears of corn that rest on the mkeka and represent the number of children in the family.

Nguzo Saba (En-GOO- zoh SAH-bah) - A term meaning seven principles in Swahili.

Nia (NEE-ah) - One of the seven principles of Kwanzaa, meaning "purpose", and celebrated on the fifth day of Kwanzaa.

Swahili (Swah-HEE-lee) - An East African language used in many parts of the continent, not linked to any one tribe and commonly referred to as Swahili.

Tamshi La Tambiko (TAM-shee La Tam-BEE-Koo) - The closing statement of the Kwanzaa Karamu.

Ujamaa (Oo-jah-MAH) - One of the seven principles of Kwanzaa meaning cooperative economics and celebrated on the fourth day of Kwanzaa.

Ujima (Oo-JEE-mah) - One of the seven principles of Kwanzaa meaning collective work and responsibility and celebrated on the third day of Kwanzaa.

Umoja (Oo-MOH-jah) - One of the seven principles of Kwanzaa and celebrated on the first day of Kwanzaa.

Zawadi (Zah-WAH-dee) - Simple gifts, usually handmade, that are meant not only to educate the children, but as a reflection of love and care on the part of the individual giving the gifts.

Selected Bibliography

Anderson, David A./ Sankofa.
  Kwanzaa: An Everyday Resource and Instructional Guide, (Gumbs & Thomas Publishers, Inc. 1992).
Copage, Eric V.
  Kwanzaa: An African-American Celebration of Culture and Cooking, (William Morrow, 1991)
Davis-Thompson, Helen.
  Let's Celebrate Kwanzaa: An Activity Book for Young Readers, (Gumbs & Thomas Publishers, Inc. 1989).
Johnson Ph.D., James W. Johnson, Ph.D., E. Frances, Slaughter, Ph.D., Ronald L.
  The Nguzo Saba and Festival of First Fruits, (Gumbs & Thomas Publishers, Inc. 1995).
Karenga, Dr. Maulana.
  Kwanzaa: A Celebration of Family, Community and Culture, Commemorative Edition, (University of Sankore Press, 1998).
McClester, Cedric.
  Kwanzaa: Everything You Always Wanted To Know But Didn't Know Where To Ask, 30th Anniversary Edition (Gumbs & Thomas Publishers, Inc. 1996).
Tukufu, Dr. Darryl S.
  A Guide Toward The Successful Development Of African-American Males (The Tukufu Group, 1997).

Ndebele painted wall facade, Republic of South Africa

Additional Kwanzaa Information

Books for Children

Banks, Valerie. *The Kwanzaa Coloring Book*, 5th Edition,
    Illustrated by Sylvia Woodward (Sala Enterprises,1991)
Bland, Margaret. *Getting Ready for Kwanzaa* (Jomar Enterprises,1985)
Cockfield, Carolyn M. *My Kwanzaa Book*, 3rd Edition (Sea Island Information Group, 1991)
Chocolate, Deborah M. Newton. *My First Kwanzaa Book*,
    Illustrated by Cal Massey (Scholastic, Inc./Just Us Books, 1992)
Chocolate, Deborah M. *Kwanzaa: A Family Affair* (Children's Press, 1990)
Copage, Eric. *A Kwanzaa Fable* (William Morrow Co., 1995)
Davis-Pinckney, Andrea. *The Seven Candles for Kwanzaa*,
    Illustrated by Brian Pinckney (Dial/Penguin Books, 1993)
Ford, Juwanda. *K is for Kwanzaa: A Kwanzaa Alphabet Book*
    Illustrated by Ken Wilson-Max (Scholastic/Cartwheel, 1997)
Grier, Ella. *Seven Days of Kwanzaa*, Illustrated by John Ward (Viking, 1997)
Holt-Goldsmith, Diane. *Celebrating Kwanzaa*,
    photography by Lawrence Migdale (Holiday House, Inc. 1993)
Johnson, Dolores. *The Children's Book of Kwanzaa*
    (Simon & Schuster/Aladdin, 1997)
Madhubuti, Safisha. *The Story of Kwanzaa: An Introduction to the*
    Origin and Tradition of Kwanzaa (Third World Press, 1989)
Robertson, Linda & Pearson, Julia. *Kwanzaa Fun*
    (Larousse Kingfisher Chamber, Inc.,1996)
Ross, Kathy. *Crafts For Kwanzaa* Illustrated by Sharon Lane Holm (Millbrook Press, 1994)
Saint-James, Synthia. The Gifts of Kwanzaa (Albert Whitman & Co., 1994)

Books for Adults

Harris, Jessica B. *A Kwanzaa Keepsake: Celebrating the Holiday with*
    New Traditions and Feasts (Simon & Schuster, 1995)
Karenga, Dr. Maulana. *Kawaida: A Communitarian African Philosophy* (University of Sankore
    Press, 1980)
Madhubuti, Haki. *Kwanzaa: A Progressive and Uplifting African American Holiday* (Third
    World Press, 1987)

Terry, Rod. *Kwanzaa: The Seven Principles* (Peter Pauper Press, Inc., 1996)
Winbrush-Riley, Dorothy. *The Complete Kwanzaa: Celebrating Our Cultural Harvest*
(HarperCollins, 1995)

Cookbooks

J.U.G.S., Inc.,Washington, DC Chapter. *Sharing Our Best* (Fundcraft)
Mitchell, Patricai B. *Soul On Rice*: African Influences On American Cooking (Historic Sims-
Mitchell House, 1993)
Shelf-Medearis, Angela. *A Kwanzaa Celebration: Festive Recipes
and Homemade Gifts From An African-American Kitchen*
(NAL Dutton, 1995)

Audio Tapes

Aremu, Aduke and Stiefel, Ben. *A Magical Musical Celebration of Kwanzaa: A Children's Musical
Play* (Gumbs & Thomas Publishers, Inc, 1995)
Blue Salim. *Celebrate Kwanzaa* (Culture Gun Productions, 1996)
Cobb, Steve and Charunduka. *Seven Principles* (Cobbala Records, 1997)
Kwanzaa Kwest Soundtrack (Konscious Kommunications, 1997)
Sala. *Kwanzaa* (Gumbs & Thomas Publishers, Inc.1990)
The Nguzo Saba: The Seven Principles of Kwanzaa (Konscious Kommunications, 1997)

Video Tapes

*African American Holiday of Kwanzaa: A Celebration of Family,
Community and Culture* (The University of Sankora Press, 1997)
Kwanzaa: An African American Celebration (Adonis Productions, 1996)
Kwanzaa Kwest (Konscious Kommunications, 1997)
The Celebration of Kwanzaa: Echos of Africa
(Che Chan Dear Productions, 1995)

African Musical Audio Tapes

OLATUNJI!: Drums Of Passion (Columbia Records/CBS, Inc.)

Interactive Multimedia CD-Rom

Kwanzaa: The First Fruits of the Harvest (Konscious Kommunications, 1997)

Jigsaw Puzzles

Kwanzaa: Family Celebration (W.B. Adams, 1996)

Shoppers' Guide for Kwanzaa Products

Below is a selected listing of community-based businesses in the United States and the Caribbean selling Kwanzaa books, celebration sets, kinaras, candles, greeting cards, audio tapes, and African fashions.

Alabama
Mahogany Books 205 20th Street N. Birmingham, AL 35203
Roots and Wings Bookstore 1345 Carter Hill Road Montgomery, AL 36106
The Culture Shop 2207C University Drive Huntsville, AL 36106

Arizona
Blackbird Gifts 130 N. Central Avenue, Suite B8 Phoenix, AZ 85004
Changing Hands Bookstore 414 S. Mill Avenue #109 Tempe, AZ 85281

Arkansas
Afrika Enterprises 707 E. Broadway West Memphis, AR 73201
Images In Black 1310 Rose Street Texarkana, AR 75502

California
Carol's Books 5964 S. Land Park Drive Sacramento, CA 95822
Conscious Books 2819 Telegraph Avenue Oakland, CA 94607
Eso Won Books 904 N. LaBrea Avenue Englewood, CA 90302-2208
Karibu 30 Jack London Square Oakland, CA 94607
Kongo Square Gallery 4334 Degnan Blvd. Los Angeles, CA 90008
The University of Sankore Press 2560 W. 54th Street Los Angeles, CA 90043

Colorado
From Slaveship to Ownership 620 E. 17th Avenue Denver, CO 80203
House of Osiris 2736 Welton Denver, CO 80205
Hue-Man Experience 911 Park Avenue W. Denver, CO 80206

Connecticut
African Treasures Collection 862 Asylum Avenue, Suite 1 Hartford, CT 06105
Asha Health & Cultural Center 691 Water Street Bridgeport, CT 06604
Dygnyti Books 828 Dixwell Avenue Hamden, CT 06514

District of Columbia
Praise to Print Bookstore 1225 W Street, SE Washington, DC 20020
Pyramid Books 2849 Georgia Avenue, NW Washington, DC 20001
Yawa Books & Gifts 2206 18th Street, NW Washington, DC 20011

Florida
Afro-In-Books-N-Things 5575 NW 7th Avenue Miami, FL 33127
Pyramid Books 544-2 Gateway Blvd. Boynton Beach, FL 33435
Tenaj Books & Gift Gallery 608 S. US 1 Fort Pierce, FL 34950
Ujamaa African Book Store 3600 W. Broward Blvd. Ft. Lauderdale, FL 33312

Georgia
African Inspired Gifts & Greetings 5878 Covington Highway Decatur, GA 30335
Afrocentric Cards & Gifts 2375 Wesley Chapel Road #10 Decatur, GA 30035
Brothers 3 Bookstore Shannon Southpark Mall 115 Shannon Southpark Union City, GA 30291
Shrine of the Black Madonna 446 Abernathy Blvd. Atlanta, GA 30310

Hawaii
Black Imani Books 98-027 Hekana #35 Aiea, HI 96701

Illinois
Afrocentric Bookstore 333 S. State Street Chicago, IL 60604
Bolaolu 1805 Grand Avenue Waukeegan, IL 60085
Motherland Art & Design 125 W. Church Champaign, IL 61820
Mother to Daughter, A Touch of Blackness 2133 S.17th Avenue Broadview, IL 60153

Indiana
African Specialty Items 3840 Marrison Place Indianapolis, IN 46226
Renaissance Books 1227 Broadway Gary, IN 46407
X-Pression 5912 N. College Avenue Indianapolis, IN 46220

Iowa
Afro Mart 3448 Martin Luther King Blvd. Des Moines, IA 50310
Campus Book Store 2300 Lincoln Way Ames, IA 50014

Kansas
IGRAA African-American Books 2219 E. 13th Street Wichita, KS 67214
Kultural Expressions 646 State Avenue Kansas City, KS 66101

Kentucky
The Learning Tree 2470 Franklin Road Russellville, KY 42276

Louisiana
Books Plus 1800 N.E. Evangeline Thrwy. Lafayette, LA 70501
Sankofa Kay's Books & Things 1707 Susek Drive Pineville, LA 71360
The Afro-American Book Stop 5700 Read Blvd #275 New Orleans, LA 70127-2665

Maryland
African World Books 1356 W. North Avenue Baltimore, MD 21217
Gallery Africa 1306 Chapel Oak Drive Capital Heights, MD 20743
Remmy's Afrikan Konnection Landover Mall Landover, MD 20785

Massachusetts
A Nubian Notion 41 Warren Street Boston, MA 02119
Treasured Legacy Copley Place, 100 Huntington Avenue Boston, MA 02116

Michigan
African World 3906 Clio Road Flint, MI 48504
Multi-Media Education 19363 Livernois Detroit, MI 48221
Shrine of the Black Madonna 13535 Livernois Detroit, MI 48238

Minnesota
Inside Africa 175 E. 5th Street, Box 12 #114 St. Paul, MN 55101
Uhuru Books 1304 E. Lake Street Minneapolis, MN 55407

Mississippi
Adhiambo Books & Gifts 3424 Robinson Street Jackson, MS 39209
The Book Gallery 647 S. Theobald Street, Suite D Jackson, MS 38701

Missouri
Afrikana 6608 Delmar Blvd. St. Louis, MO 63130
J. Gillyard Treasures 9977 Lewis & Clark Blvd. St. Louis, MO 63136
The Culture Shop 1715 Dunn Road Florissant, MO 63033

Nebraska
Afro American Bookstore 3226 Lake Street Omaha, NB 68111
First World 7400 Dodge Street Omaha, NB 68114

Nevada
Afrocentric, Inc. 12002 Himalaya Street Reno, NV 89506-1508
Final Call Books & Tapes 1402 D Street Las Vegas, NV 89106

New Jersey
African Kultural Village 183 Martin Luther King Drive Jersey City, NJ 07305
Kujichagulia 155 Ellison Street Paterson, NJ 07505
Princess Cultural Effects 494 Main Street East Orange, NJ 07018
Tunde Dada-House of Africa, Inc. 356 Main Street Orange, NJ 07050

New York
4W-Circle of Art & Enterprise 704 Fulton Street Brooklyn, NY 11207
African Paradise 27 West 125th Street New York, NY 10027
Black Books Plus 702 Amsterdam Avenue New York, NY 10025
Cultural Expressions, Inc. P.O. Box 373 New York, NY 10039
Dee's Card N Wedding Service 480 Lenox Avenue New York, NY 10037
Fatou's Fashion Designs 2530 8th Avenue New York, NY 10030
Gumbs & Thomas Publishers, Inc. P.O.Box 381 New York, NY 10039
Harambee Books & Crafts 31 St. Paul Mall Buffalo, NY 14209
Homeland 122 West 27th Street, 8th floor New York, NY 10001
Indigo Images, Inc. 515 Manhattan Avenue New York, NY 10027
Nigerian Fabrics & Fashions 501 Fulton Street Brooklyn, NY 11217
Pope's Gifts & Accessory Shop 445 W. 125th Street New York, NY 10027
Source International Technology Corp., 939 East 156th Street Bronx, NY 10455

North Carolina
Heritage House 901 S. Kings Drive Charlotte, NC 28204
Quail Ridge Books 3522 Wade Avenue Raleigh, NC 27607
Sharon's Gifts & Accessories 1726 Washington Street New Bern, NC 28560
Special Occasions 112 N Martin Luther King Drive Winston-Salem, NC 27001

Ohio
A Cultural Exchange 12621 Larchmare Blvd. Cleveland, OH 44120
Malikah International Boutique 17122 Chagrin Blvd. Shaker Heights, OH 44120
Timbuktu Book Shop 5508 Superior Avenue Cleveland, OH 44103

Oklahoma
Paperback Connection 5120 N. Classon Blvd. Oklahoma City, OK 73118
SJ Book Shoppe 700 N. Greenwood Avenue Tulsa, OK 74106-0706

Oregon
All About Knowledge 5009 N. Maryland Avenue Portland, OR 97217
Reflections 446 NE Killingsworth Street Portland, OR 97211

Pennsylvania
Afro Mission 104 S. 13th Street Philadelphia, PA 19107
Ashanti Potpourri 7618 Frankstown Avenue Pittsburgh, PA 15208
Aya Boutique 265 S. 44th Street Philadelphia, PA 19104
Chic Afrique Gallery 2, 2nd Level 10th and Market Street Philadelphia, PA 19107
The Nia House 2822 Wilson Parkway Harrisburg, PA 17104

Rhode Island
The Jelly Bean Tree Gift Shop 106 Reservoir Avenue Providence, RI 02907

South Carolina
Armeco's 318 Sycamore Drive North Augusta, SC 29841
Mirror Images Books & Toys 946 Orleans Road, Suite B3 Charleston, SC 29407

Tennessee
Afrikan Emporium 3984 Elvis Presley Blvd. Memphis, TN 38116
African-American Cultural Alliance 3520 W. Hamilton Road Nashville, TN 37218
Regina's African Village Choo Choo Shuttle Park South, 1394 Market Street Chattanooga, TN 37402
Sherman's Books 5625 Flowering Peach Drive Memphis, TN 38115

Texas
Black Images Book Bazaar 230 Wynnewood Village Dallas, TX 75224
Culturally Correct 201 E. 24th Street Tyler, TX 75702

Utah
Amiti Imports 733 E. Springview Salt Lake City, UT 84106
Harambee 272 E. 900 South Salt Lake City, UT 84111

Vermont
Authentic African Imports RR 2, Box 2055, North Greenbush Road Charlotte, VT 05445
Kemp Krafts 288 Flynn Avenue # 20 Burlington, VT 05401-5374

Virginia
African Traders Unlimited 1800 W. Mercury Blvd., Coliseum Mall, B2 Hampton, VA 23666
Cooks Books & More 610 N. Sheppard Street Richmond, VA 23221
Jeanette Enterprises 1526 Edgelawn Circle, Suite B Richmond, VA 23231
Liberation Bookstore 238 N. Henry Alexandria, VA 22314
Unique Boutique 1209 Nelwood Drive Richmond, VA 23231

Washington
Blackbird Books 1316 E Pike Street Seattle, WA 98122
Know Thyself Afrikan Book Center 317 S. 11th Street Tacoma,WA 98402-3501

West Virginia
Kuumba Unlimited 625 6th Street Huntington, WV 25701
The Gift Shoppe 152 Willey Street Morgantown, WV 26505

Wisconsin
African Center 1912 W. Hampton Avenue Milwaukee, WI 53209
Baskets On Occasion 2821 N. 4th Street, Suite 53 Milwaukee, WI 53212

United States Virgin Islands
Education Station Ltd. Wheatley Center #16 St.Thomas,VI 00802
Village Life P.O.Box 942 Christiansted, St. Croix, VI 00821